T

The Art of Cakes

The Art of Cakes

Noga Hitron

Photography by Matt Cohen

STERLING

New York / London
www.sterlingpublishing.com

Design and layout by Ariane Rybski
Edited by Shoshana Brickman
Photography by Matt Cohen

STERLING and the distinctive Sterling logo are registered trademarks of
Sterling Publishing Co., Inc.

Library of Congress Cataloging-in-Publication Data

Hitron, Noga.
The art of cakes : colorful cake designs for the creative baker / Noga Hitron ;
photography by Matt Cohen.
p. cm.
Includes index.
ISBN 978-1-4027-6124-9
1. Cake. 2. Cake decorating. I. Cohen, Matt. II. Title.

TX771.H585 2008
641.8'6539--dc22

2008001582

10 9 8 7 6 5 4 3 2 1

Published by Sterling Publishing Co., Inc.
387 Park Avenue South, New York, NY 10016
Penn Publishing Ltd.
1 Yehuda Halevi St., Tel Aviv, Israel 65135
© 2008 by Penn Publishing Ltd.
Distributed in Canada by Sterling Publishing
c/o Canadian Manda Group, 165 Dufferin Street
Toronto, Ontario, Canada M6K 3H6
Distributed in the United Kingdom by GMC Distribution Services
Castle Place, 166 High Street, Lewes, East Sussex, England BN7 1XU
Distributed in Australia by Capricorn Link (Australia) Pty. Ltd.
P.O. Box 704, Windsor, NSW 2756, Australia

Printed in China
All rights reserved

Sterling ISBN 978-1-4027-6124-9

For information about custom editions, special sales, premium and
corporate purchases, please contact Sterling Special Sales
Department at 800-805-5489 or specialsales@sterlingpublishing.com.

Table of Contents

Note from the Author

There are so many occasions to celebrate—birthdays and graduations, weddings and anniversaries, holidays and surprise parties. Cakes are part of all of these celebrations, and having a really beautiful cake—one that you've made in your very own kitchen—can make a special occasion extraordinary.

That's the inspiration behind this book—a guide to creating vibrant, colorful and unique cakes that will bring "miles of smiles" to the faces of every one of your guests. Anyone with a little experience in cake decorating can create these cakes. Just choose an occasion, equip yourself with some basic tools, and set your imagination free.

Some of the cakes, such as "Colorful and Crazy" and "Happy Birthday to You," are relatively simple. They require basic decorating tools and are great starter projects if you are just discovering the world of cake decorating. Other cakes, such as "Happily Ever After" and "Beautiful Baby Birthday," require a little more expertise, and some advanced planning. These cakes are perfect for more experienced cake designers, but are accessible to anyone who has the right equipment, and plenty of enthusiasm.

I came to the baker's kitchen from the artist's studio. After spending several years studying and working in graphic design, I found that cake decorating was a perfect way to combine my love of aesthetics with my passion for baking.

I used lots of imagination when I created the designs for this book, and I recommend you do the same. Don't be afraid to experiment with different color combinations, and to adapt the designs to suit your style, taste, and occasion. Although there are detailed instructions for all of the steps, there are also many opportunities to improvise.

It's wonderful to watch the mixture of wonder and happiness on a person's face when they receive one of my cakes. I am sure you'll feel the same thrill when you present your cakes to family and friends. Be sure to take lots of photos—of your cakes, and of your guests' reactions.

Happy designing,

Noga Hitron

Basic Recipes, Techniques, and Tools

Basic Recipes

Cakes

The best type of cake for decorating is firm and moist, so that it can be cut and shaped without crumbling. The designs in this book are best suited to cakes that are least 3 inches high, unless otherwise stated. You can increase the height of a cake pan by lining it with parchment paper, so that the paper extends beyond the upper rim of the pan. The recipes below yield enough batter for one 10 x 3-inch round cake. Adjust the quantities according to the size of cake you want for your design. Also, be sure to adjust the baking time according to your oven, and to the size of your cake. Deeper cakes will require a little more time to bake; shallower cakes will require a little less time.

Madeira Sponge Cake

- 2 cups butter or soft margarine, room temperature
- 2 cups sugar
- 9 medium eggs
- 4 tablespoons milk or citrus juice
- 4 ¼ cups all-purpose flour
- 2 ½ teaspoons baking powder

1. Preheat oven to 325°F. Grease a 10-inch round cake pan and line with parchment paper. Make sure the parchment paper extends beyond the top rim of the pan, so that the cake has room to rise.

2. Cream the butter and sugar until light and fluffy, about 5 minutes if you are using an electric mixer. Add the eggs one at a time, beating well after each addition. Add the milk and mix. In a separate bowl, sift the flour and baking powder. Blend the mixtures together using a wooden spoon, then beat until smooth and glossy.

3. Pour the batter into the prepared pan and level the top with a spatula.

4. Place the cake in the center of the oven and bake for 1¾ to 2 hours, or until a toothpick inserted into the center comes out clean.

5. Cool the cake for 30 minutes, then turn it out onto a wire rack and set aside until completely cool.

Chocolate Cake

- 2 cups cocoa
- 2 cups boiling water
- 1¾ cups butter or margarine, room temperature
- 3½ cups sugar
- 6 eggs
- 2 teaspoons rum extract
- 3½ cups all-purpose flour
- 4 teaspoons baking powder

1. Preheat oven to 350°F. Grease a 10-inch round cake pan and line with parchment paper. Make sure the parchment paper extends beyond the top rim of the pan, so that the cake has room to rise.

2. Mix the cocoa and water until blended, then set aside for 5 minutes to cool.

3. Cream the butter and sugar until light and fluffy, about 5 minutes if you are using an electric mixer. Add the eggs and rum extract, and beat thoroughly. In a separate bowl, sift the flour and baking powder. Add the flour mixture to the creamed mixture, alternating with the cocoa mixture, and beating well after each addition.

4. Pour the batter into the prepared pan and level the top with a spatula.

5. Place the cake in the middle of the oven and bake for about 50 minutes, or until a toothpick inserted in the center comes out clean.

6. Cool the cake for 30 minutes, then turn it out onto a wire rack and set aside until completely cool.

Fruity Cake

- 1¾ cups butter or margarine, room temperature
- 4 cups brown sugar
- 6 eggs
- 1 cup oil
- 2 teaspoons vanilla extract
- 6 cups all-purpose flour
- 2 teaspoons salt
- 2 teaspoons baking soda
- 4 heaping teaspoons cinnamon
- Two 29-ounce cans peach or pear halves in light syrup
- 8 ounces coarsely ground pecans

1. Preheat oven to 350°F. Grease a 10-inch round cake pan and line with parchment paper. Make sure the parchment paper extends beyond the top rim of the pan, so that the cake has room to rise.

2. Cream the butter and sugar until light and fluffy, about 5 minutes if you are using an electric mixer. Add the eggs, oil, and vanilla extract and beat thoroughly. In a separate bowl, combine the flour, salt, baking soda, and cinnamon. Drain the peaches, reserving the syrup from one can. Add the flour mixture to the creamed mixture, alternating with the peaches, and beating well after each addition. Add pecans and mix thoroughly.

3. Pour the batter into the prepared pan and level the top with a spatula.

4. Place the cake in the middle of the oven and bake for about 50 minutes, or until a toothpick inserted into the center comes out clean.

5. Pour the reserved syrup over the cake while it is still warm. Let the cake cool for 1 hour, then turn it out onto a wire rack and set aside until completely cool.

Buttercream

Buttercream, jam, chocolate spread, or any other sweet smooth spread provides a delicious surface for applying the rolled fondant. You can use a variety of ready-made spreads sold at grocery and specialty stores, or follow the recipe below.

Makes 3 cups

- 1 cup butter or soft margarine
- 1 teaspoon vanilla extract
- 4 cups sifted confectioners' sugar
- 2 tablespoons milk

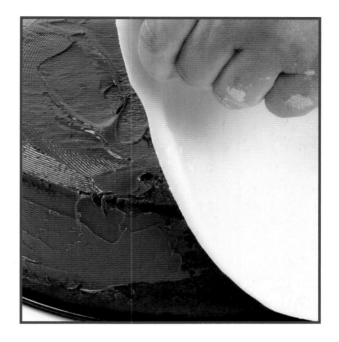

1. Cream the butter with an electric mixer. Add the vanilla and mix well. Sift sugar into the bowl, one cup at a time, while beating on medium speed. Scrape the sides and bottom of the bowl often.

2. When all the sugar has been added, the icing will appear dry. Add the milk and beat on medium speed until light and fluffy.

3. Refrigerate and store in an airtight container for up to two weeks. Re-whip before using.

Rolled Fondant

I recommend using ready-made rolled fondant (sugarpaste), available at specialty stores and through catalogs. Rolled fondant usually comes in white or off-white, but is also sold pre-colored. To prevent sticking when working with rolled fondant, always work on a dry surface that is lightly covered with cornstarch.

You will find that the quantities of rolled fondant suggested in this book are quite generous. This is because working with small quantities of fondant is difficult, especially when kneading in color. Leftover rolled fondant that is tightly wrapped in plastic wrap and kept in an airtight container can be stored for several months. Keep rolled fondant in a cool, dry place. Do not refrigerate or freeze.

If the rolled fondant you are working with is particularly hard, try heating it in the microwave for a few seconds (no more than 5 seconds at a time) to soften it.

To prepare your own rolled fondant, follow the recipe below.

Makes 2 pounds

- 1 tablespoon unflavored gelatin
- 3 tablespoons cold water
- ½ cup liquid glucose
- 1 tablespoon glycerin
- 2 tablespoons solid vegetable shortening
- 8 cups sifted confectioners' sugar

1. Put the gelatin in the water and let stand until thick. Place the gelatin mixture into the top of a double boiler and gently heat until dissolved. Add the glucose and glycerin, and mix well. Stir in the shortening and remove from the heat just before it melts completely. Allow the mixture to cool slightly.

2. Place 4 cups of confectioners' sugar in a bowl and make a well. Pour the gelatin mixture into the well and stir, mixing in the sugar until the stickiness disappears. Knead in the remaining sugar until the fondant does not stick to your hands.

3. Tightly wrap in plastic wrap and store in an airtight container. Place in a cool, dry place. Do not refrigerate or freeze.

Modeling Paste

Several shapes and figures in this book require the use of modeling paste that is flexible and firm, and that holds its shape when you are working with it and when it is dry. This can be made by adding tragacanth gum, a natural thickener, to rolled fondant. Carboxyl Methyl Cellulose (CMC) is a chemical alternative to tragacanth gum. CMC is cheaper and can be stored for longer than tragacanth gum. Both are available at specialty stores and through catalogs. To prepare 1 pound of modeling paste, put 2 teaspoons of gum tragacanth or CMC onto a dry surface that is lightly covered with cornstarch. Knead into 1 pound of rolled fondant until smooth. Store in an airtight container for at least 1 hour before use.

If you find that your modeling paste isn't stable enough—for example, when shaping figures that are particularly tall, or shapes that are particularly thin—simply knead add a little more gum tragacanth or CMC into the modeling paste.

When possible, I recommend adding color to the rolled fondant prior to adding the tragacanth gum or CMC, as rolled fondant is easier to knead then modeling paste. However, colors become faded after the addition of tragacanth gum and CMC, so you may need to add extra color afterwards as well.

As with the rolled fondant, the quantities of modeling paste suggested for the designs in this book are quite generous. Leftover modeling paste that is tightly wrapped in plastic wrap and kept in an airtight container can be stored for several months. Keep modeling paste in a cool, dry place. Do not refrigerate or freeze.

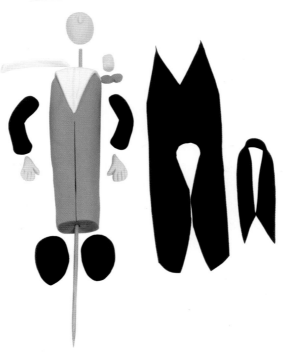

Royal Icing

Royal icing is used for piping letters, dots, and other decorations. It can be made with fresh egg whites or meringue powder, which is available at specialty stores and through catalogs.

In general, three consistencies of royal icing are used for decorating. Thin consistency royal icing resembles thick cream or syrup. To test this consistency, draw a knife through the royal icing and count to ten. If the mark disappears when you reach ten, you have the right consistency. Medium consistency royal icing resembles sour cream. You can test this consistency by using a spoon to draw up a peak in the icing. If the icing forms a soft peak that gently folds back into the icing, you have the right consistency. Thick consistency royal icing resembles stiffly beaten egg whites. This consistency should be stiff enough to hold a sharp peak.

The recipes in this book require thin consistency royal icing, unless otherwise stated. Conduct the 10-second test to check the consistency of royal icing. If the icing is too thin, simply add a little confectioners' sugar. If it is too thick, simply add a little water. Royal icing made from egg whites can be stored in the refrigerator for up to three days in an airtight container. Royal icing made from meringue powder can be stored at room temperature for up to two weeks in an airtight container.

Makes 1½ cups

- 1 large egg white
- 1½ cups sifted confectioners' sugar
- 1 tablespoon water

1. Place the egg white and confectioners' sugar in a mixing bowl. Beat on low speed for 10 minutes, until the mixture has the consistency of thick cream or syrup.

2. Test the consistency by drawing a knife through the icing and counting. If the mark disappears by the time you reach 10, you have the right consistency. Add water to thin, or confectioners' sugar to thicken.

3. Store in an airtight container until ready to use.

If you are using meringue powder instead of egg white, put 1 tablespoon of powder into 2 tablespoons of water and stir until the powder is completely blended and free of lumps. Add confectioners' sugar and beat, as described above.

Techniques

Preparing the cake

I recommend lining your cake pan with parchment paper before pouring in the batter. This helps the cake come out of the pan smoothly, and with a minimal amount of crumbling. Also, by allowing the parchment paper to extend beyond the top rim of the pan, the cake will have more room to rise. After the cake has cooled thoroughly, level it using a sharp serrated knife and turn it upside down. Do not place the cake directly on a work surface when decorating, because moving a decorated cake can be difficult. Instead, work directly on the cake board, on a thick piece of cardboard, or on the serving tray.

Adding color

I recommend using concentrated gel colors, available at specialty stores and through catalogs. Gel colors are nontoxic and don't leave an aftertaste. They come in a large variety of colors, which can be mixed together to create even more variety.

Store-bought rolled fondant is usually white or off-white, although it can also be bought pre-colored. If you are adding the color yourself, dip a toothpick into the color gel and add to the rolled fondant. Knead until the color is evenly blended, adding a little bit of gel each time until you have the desired shade. You may want to wear gloves when kneading in the gel color, as it can stain your hands.

When tinting modeling paste, keep in mind that the presence of tragacanth gum or CMC means you will need more gel color to get the desired shade. If possible, add color to the rolled fondant before adding the tragacanth gum or CMC, as it will be easier to knead at this stage.

To tint royal icing, dip a toothpick into the color gel and add a little at a time to the royal icing. Mix with a spatula, adding gel until you have the desired shade.

To tint sugar for making sugar molding, mix a little gel color with 2–3 teaspoons of water. Add 1 cup of sugar and mix well, until the sugar is evenly colored and has a texture resembling wet sand.

Covering the cake

When using rolled fondant to cover cakes, it should be rolled to a thickness of ¼ inch. To determine the area of fondant you will need to cover a cake, measure the sides and the top of the cake across the center. Add 1 inch to each side, for trimming. For example, a 10 x 3-inch cake will require rolled fondant that is 18 inches in diameter.

Once the rolled fondant is the correct thickness and size, place the rolling pin in the middle of the rolled fondant. Loosely fold one half of the fondant over the rolling pin and carefully lift the rolling pin, with the fondant, above the center of the cake. Gently lay one half of the fondant onto the cake, adjusting so that it completely covers one side of the cake (Figure A). Lay the other half of the fondant over the other side of the cake. Gently smooth the fondant with your hands, starting at the top and working around the sides, so that the excess rolled fondant is at the base of the cake. Trim away the excess using a pizza cutter or sharp knife.

Choosing a cake board

Styrofoam or corrugated cardboard cake boards of various shapes and sizes are available at specialty stores or through catalogs. Some of the designs in this book use cake boards that are covered with paper or foil; others call for a rolled fondant covering. When covering a cake board in rolled fondant, the fondant should be rolled to a thickness of ⅛ inch and left to dry overnight before positioning the cake.

Working with rolled fondant and modeling paste

Always work on a clean, dry surface when rolling out or shaping rolled fondant or modeling paste. Use cornstarch to prevent the material from sticking to your hands or to the work surface. To stick pieces of rolled fondant or modeling paste together, apply a little water using a small paintbrush. Royal icing is often used as a "glue" for affixing figures and objects made from modeling paste that have dried.

Supporting figures

Relatively light figures can usually be supported using pieces of dry spaghetti. This is the safest type of support, because it is edible and not too sharp (Figure B). However, some designs require sturdier supports, such as toothpicks, floristry wire, or wooden skewers. In such cases, please make sure that the people who are serving the cake are aware that these materials are in the cake.

Storing the cake

Decorated cakes should be stored in a dry, cool place away from direct heat or sunlight. Do not refrigerate or freeze.

Tools

Bone tool is used for making indents in rolled fondant and modeling paste. The back of a paintbrush can sometimes be used as a substitute.

Cutters are used to cut flowers, circles, stars, and other shapes. In many cases, objects such as glass rims, plates, baking pans, or templates can be used as substitutes.

Decorating bags, couplers, and tips are used for piping royal icing. You can make your own decorating bags out of parchment paper, or purchase ready-made bags.

Design wheeler is used to create a "seam" on modeling paste. You can also use a toothpick to mark a seam, although this requires a steady hand and patience.

Floristry wire is useful for supporting flowers and other small figures. It is available at craft stores and through catalogs.

Frill cutter is used for cutting frilled edges.

Open-curve crimper, also called a single closed scallop crimper, is used to create textured trims around the cakes. Crimpers come in a variety of shapes and sizes.

Paintbrushes are used to apply water for affixing rolled fondant and modeling paste, or for painting small details such as eyes, eyebrows, and mouths.

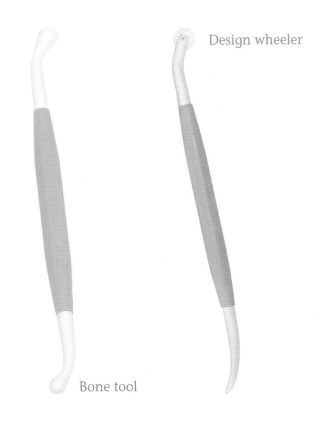

Design wheeler

Bone tool

Flower cutter

Leaf cutter

Parchment paper is used for lining baking pans, and as a surface for drawing figures made from royal icing.

Pieces of foam are useful for supporting figures as they dry.

Pizza cutter is used to trim rolled fondant. A regular knife can also be used, but the moving edge of the pizza cutter allows for a smoother cut.

Rolling pins are used for rolling out modeling paste and rolled fondant. Lined rolling pins are used to create textured surfaces.

Sharp knives are used for cutting various shapes. Use a serrated knife for trimming cakes and a straight knife for cutting shapes.

Sticks of dry spaghetti are the best type of support because they are edible and not too sharp. However, they are not strong enough to support all figures, and in some cases, toothpicks, floristry wire, or wooden skewers are required.

Toothpicks are perfect for making small marks and to frill edges. In some cases, they are also used as supports, although care must be taken because they are sharp. Be sure to choose high quality, rounded toothpicks that don't splinter.

Wooden skewers are used for supporting large, heavy figures. Regular wooden skewers are sufficient in most cases, unless otherwise stated.

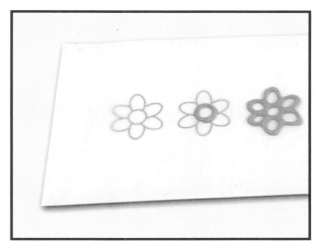

Parchment paper

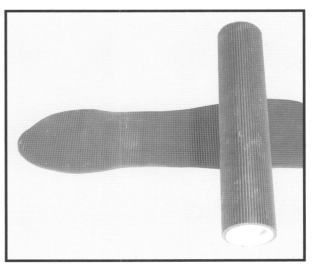

Lined rolling pin

23

Cake Designs

Cheerful Chicks

This cheerful cake is perfect for baby birthdays and other sunny celebrations. Use your imagination to create different types of figures for placing around the top, such as boats, butterflies, or ladybugs.

Materials

* 8-inch round cake
* 1½ cups buttercream or smooth cream
* 2 pounds 2 ounces rolled fondant, divided and tinted to make:
  * 10 ounces green
  * 1½ pounds white
* 13 ounces modeling paste, divided and tinted to make:
  * 11 ounces dark blue
  * 2 ounces light blue
* 2 batches of royal icing (page 18), divided into equal parts and tinted to make:
  * orange
  * yellow
  * blue
  * green

Tools

* Template (page 98)
* Parchment paper
* Several decorating bags and couplers
* #2 round decorating tips
* 10 toothpicks
* Rolling pin
* 9-inch round cake board
* Pizza cutter or sharp knife
* Open-curve crimper
* 1-inch and 6-inch round cutters

Two days in advance

Chicks

1. Trace 10 chicks onto white paper, using the template on page 98. Place parchment paper over the white paper and re-trace the chicks using the orange royal icing. Wait 10 minutes, then fill with yellow royal icing. Wait an hour, then pipe yellow royal icing to make wings and blue royal icing to make eyes. You will need 10 chicks for this cake, but I recommend making a few extra in case any break while you are assembling the cake. Set aside to dry for 12 hours (Figure A).

2. When the chicks are completely dry, carefully remove from the parchment paper and turn over. Using a few drops of yellow royal icing, affix a toothpick on the flat side of each chick, so that the end of the toothpick extends by $1/2$ inch from the bottom of the chick. Decorate with orange, yellow, and blue royal icing, so that both sides of the chick are identical. Set aside to dry for 12 hours.

One day in advance

Cake board

3. Thinly roll out the green rolled fondant and cover the cake board, trimming the edges with the pizza cutter. Set aside to dry for at least 12 hours.

Preparing the cake

4. Level the cake and turn it upside down onto the cake board. Spread buttercream over the top and sides of the cake. Roll out the white rolled fondant and wrap the cake, using the pizza cutter to cut away excess. Crimp an S-shaped pattern along the upper edge of the cake by alternating the position of the open-curve crimper each time you crimp, and leaving a small space between each pair of crimps.

5. Roll out 7 ounces of dark blue modeling paste into a 26 x 2-inch strip. Roll some light blue modeling paste into thin sausages and bend to form W-shapes. Place on the dark blue modeling paste and gently roll to inlay. Straighten one length of the strip using the pizza

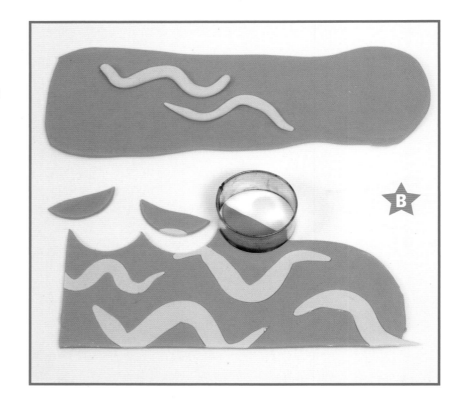

cutter. To make the waved edge along the other length, cut out semi-circles using the 1-inch round cutter (Figure B). Affix the strip along the base of the cake using a little water.

6. Roll out the remaining dark blue modeling paste and inlay W-shaped strips of light blue modeling paste. Cut out a circle using the 6-inch round cutter and place on top of the cake, using a little water to stick.

7. Use the green royal icing to pipe small balls around the base of the cake, and around the circle on the top of the cake. Use the blue royal icing to decorate the crimped edge of the cake. Insert the chicks on the top of the cake, placing them close together and facing the same direction (Figure C).

Beautiful Baby Birthday

This cake is delicate and sweet—just like the new lives it celebrates.

Materials

* 10-inch round cake and 6-inch round cake
* 3 cups buttercream or smooth cream of your choice
* 4 pounds white rolled fondant
* 1 pound 12 ounces modeling paste, divided and tinted to make:
  * 15 ounces light yellow
  * 2 ounces peach
  * 4 1/2 ounces light blue
  * 2 ounces light green
  * 2 1/2 ounces light pink
  * 2 ounces skin color
  * Tiny amounts of yellow and dark pink (optional)
* 2 batches of royal icing (page 18), divided into equal parts and tinted to make:
  * light peach
  * white

Tools

* Template (page 98)
* Parchment paper
* 2 decorating bags and couplers
* #2 round decorating tip
* 22 toothpicks, plus extra for decorating
* Rolling pin
* Miniature and medium flower plunger cutter
* Sponge
* Bone tool
* Veined leaf plunger cutter
* Small paintbrush
* Brown, red, and blue gel food colors
* 12-inch square cake board
* Pizza cutter or sharp knife
* Open-curve crimper
* 7-inch cardboard round
* Frill cutter
* Small round cutter
* 1 yard peach organza ribbon

Two days in advance

Hearts

1. Trace 16 hearts onto white paper, using the template on page 98. Place the parchment paper over the white paper and re-trace the hearts using the light peach royal icing. Wait 10 minutes, then fill in with white royal icing. You will need 16 hearts for this cake, but I recommend making a few extra in case any break while you are assembling the cake. Set aside to dry for 12 hours.

2. When the hearts are completely dry, carefully remove from the parchment paper and turn over. Using a few drops of white royal icing, affix a toothpick on the flat side of each heart so that the end of the toothpick extends by 1/2 inch from the bottom of the heart. Pipe the outline of the heart onto the back using light peach royal icing. Wait 10 minutes, then fill in with white royal icing, so that both sides of the heart are identical. Set aside to dry for 12 hours.

One day in advance

Flowers

3. Separately roll out the light yellow, peach, and light blue modeling paste. Using the medium flower plunger cutter, cut out 10 flowers from each color. To frill the flower petals, gently roll a toothpick along the edges of each flower, one petal at a time. Place each frilled flower on the sponge and gently press in the center with the bone tool, so that the petals protrude. Remove from the sponge and set aside to dry for 12 hours (Figure A).

A

Leaves

4. Thinly roll out the light green modeling paste. Cut out 10 leaves using the veined leaf plunger cutter. Make a gentle bend in each leaf and set aside to dry for 12 hours (Figure B).

Bunnies

5. To make the body, roll 1½ ounces of light blue modeling paste into a large teardrop shape. Make two indents at the base for the legs. Shape two pieces of light blue modeling paste into cones and press into the indents, using a little water to stick. Use a toothpick to mark the belly button and toes. Roll two small teardrop shapes for the arms, and stick onto the sides of the body (Figure C).

6. To make the head, roll 1 ounce of light blue modeling paste into a teardrop shape. Form the ears by cutting a vertical line from the top of the teardrop and extending about ½ of the way down. Gently shape each ear and twist outwards. Indent the front of each ear using the bone tool. Use a toothpick to mark the eyes and mouth, and use a tiny

ball of light pink modeling paste for the nose. Set aside to dry for 12 hours (Figure D).

7. Repeat Steps 5 and 6 with the light pink modeling paste to make the other bunny.

32

Babies

8. Using the skin color modeling paste, make two teardrop shapes for the bodies. (You can actually use any color modeling paste for the bodies, as they are covered completely with the blanket.) Make two balls for the faces, gently pressing the middle of each ball to form a slightly concave surface. Shape each hand by flattening a tiny ball of modeling paste. Cut out a thumb using a sharp knife and mark the fingers. Shape tiny balls for the nose and ears, and affix using water. Paint on eyes, eyebrows, and mouths using the gel food colors. Add a tiny piece of yellow modeling paste to each face for hair. Use the miniature flower plunger cutter to cut a pink flower and place on one baby's head. Set aside to dry for 1 hour (Figures E–F).

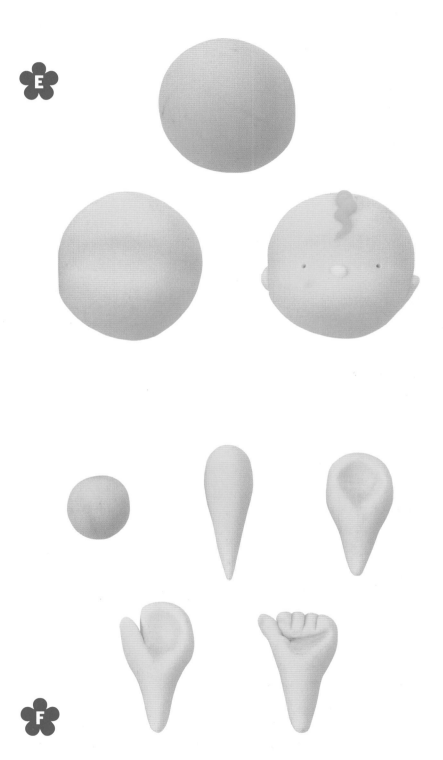

33

Preparing the cake

9. Level the larger cake and turn it upside down onto the cake board. Spread buttercream over the top and sides of the cake. Roll out 2½ pounds of white rolled fondant and wrap the cake, using the pizza cutter to cut away the excess. Crimp along the upper edge of the cake using the open-curve crimper.

10. Level the smaller cake and turn it upside down onto the cardboard round. Cover with buttercream and wrap with the remaining white rolled fondant. Crimp along the upper edge using the open-curve crimper.

11. Place the smaller cake on top of the larger cake, leaving the cardboard round between the two cakes. Set aside for 1 hour to dry.

12. Place the babies' bodies side-by-side and centered on the upper cake. To make the pillow, shape some light yellow modeling paste into a small cylinder shape. Use your thumb to press shallow indents for the heads. Stick the pillow onto the surface of the cake, just above the bodies. Place the babies' heads on the pillow, using a little water to stick.

13. To make the blanket, roll out 3 ounces of light yellow modeling paste into a square. Use a sharp knife to straighten one side of the square and trim the other three sides using the frill cutter. Gently roll a toothpick along the frilled sides, to thin and frill (Figure G). Lay the blanket over the bodies, placing the straight edge under the babies' chins and folding it over. Decorate the blanket with tiny dots of light peach royal icing.

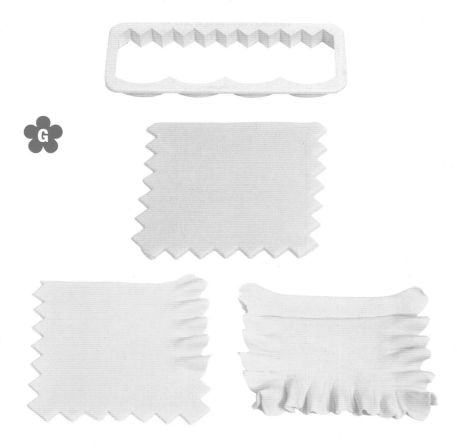

G

14. Place the bunnies on the top of the upper cake, using water to stick (Figure H). Decorate the crimped edges of both cakes by piping white royal icing. Wait 10 minutes, then pipe light peach royal icing over the white royal icing.

15. Insert the prepared hearts around the upper cake at regular intervals. Use the light peach royal icing to pipe small hearts around the upper cake, and to pipe a trim of small balls around the base of the upper cake.

16. Place the prepared flowers and leaves along the top of the lower cake, using royal icing to stick.

17. To create the frill at the bottom of the lower cake, roll out some light yellow modeling paste into a strip with a width of 1 inch. The total length of the frill will be 32 inches, but it is easier to work in smaller sections that are 3 or 4 inches long, affixing them as you go. Cut a straight edge along one length of the strip. Use the frill cutter to cut the other length, then gently

roll a toothpick to frill. Affix the frilled strips along the bottom of the lower cake, using a little water to stick.

18. Affix the ribbon around the center of the lower cake using a few drops of light peach royal icing and pipe small hearts along the ribbon. Pipe a trim of small balls along the top of the yellow frill using the light peach royal icing.

Colorful and Crazy

Plenty of occasions call for a cake—this vivid and bright design can liven up every one of them with a delicious touch of colorful craziness.

Materials

* 10-inch round cake and 6-inch round cake
* 3 cups buttercream or smooth cream
* 3 pounds 2 ounces rolled fondant, divided and tinted to make:
  * 2½ pounds green
  * 7 ounces blue
  * 1 pound orange
  * 2 ounces yellow
* 12 ounces modeling paste, divided and tinted to make:
  * 2 ounces red
  * 6 ounces yellow
  * 4 ounces blue
* 1 batch of royal icing (page 18), divided into equal parts and tinted to make:
  * blue
  * yellow

Tools

* Rolling pin
* Templates (page 99)
* 2 wooden skewers
* 12-inch square cake board
* Pizza cutter or sharp knife
* Open-curve crimper
* 7-inch cardboard round
* 2-inch crinkled round cutter
* 2 decorating bags and couplers
* #2 round decorating tip

One day in advance

Hearts

1. Thickly roll out the red modeling paste and cut out two hearts using the template on page 99. Insert the wooden skewers halfway into each heart, and set aside to dry for 12 hours (Figure A).

Preparing the cake

2. Level the larger cake and turn it upside down onto the cake board. Spread buttercream over the top and sides of the cake. Roll out the green rolled fondant and wrap the cake, using the pizza cutter to cut away the excess. Using the open-curve crimper, crimp along the upper edge of the cake.

3. Roll the blue rolled fondant into a 32-inch sausage and wrap around the base of the cake, using water to stick. Crimp the fondant using the open-curve crimper.

4. Level the smaller cake and turn it upside down onto the cardboard round. Cover with buttercream and wrap with the orange rolled fondant, cutting away the excess. Crimp along the upper edge using the open-curve crimper.

5. Center the smaller cake on top of the larger cake, leaving the cardboard round between the two cakes. Set aside to dry for 1 hour.

6. Roll out the yellow rolled fondant and cut a circle using the crinkled round cutter. Place on top of the upper cake, using a little water to stick (Figure B). Shape the yellow modeling paste into 30 large teardrop shapes and place side-by-side at the base of the upper cake, using a little water to stick (Figure C).

7. Use the blue royal icing to pipe spirals on the green cake, and to decorate the crimped edge. Use the yellow royal icing to pipe spirals and dots on the orange cake, and to decorate the crimped edge.

8. Roll out the blue modeling paste. Using the templates on page 99, cut out several stars of various sizes and affix around the lower cake, using a little water to stick. Insert the hearts into the center of the upper cake.

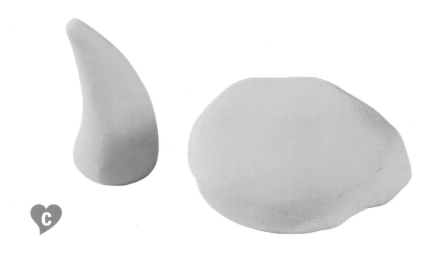

38

Clowning Around

You'll bring the circus to your table with this adorable clown cake.

Materials

* 8-inch round cake
* 1½ cups buttercream or smooth cream
* 2 pounds 6 ounces rolled fondant, divided and tinted to make:
  * 10 ounces orange
  * 1½ pounds white
  * 4 ounces green
* 1 pound 7 ounces modeling paste, divided and tinted to make:
  * 3 ounces red
  * 2 ounces yellow
  * 9 ounces orange
  * 3 ounces blue
  * 2 ounces pink
  * 1 ounce white
  * 2 ounces skin color
  * 1 ounce green
* 1 batch of white royal icing (page 18)

Tools

* Rolling pin
* 10-inch square cake board
* Pizza cutter or sharp knife
* Bone tool
* Small flower cutter
* 2-inch piece of dry spaghetti
* Open-curve crimper
* 5-inch crinkled round cutter
* Frill cutter
* Decorating bag and coupler
* #2 decorating tip

One day in advance

Cake Board

1. Thinly roll out the orange rolled fondant and cover the cake board, using the pizza cutter to trim the edges. Set aside to dry for at least 12 hours.

Clown figure

2. To make the body, roll 2 ounces of red modeling paste into a cone. Make two small indents near the bottom using the bone tool. To make the legs, roll some yellow modeling paste into two sausage shapes. Press a thin sausage of orange modeling paste onto each leg and roll gently to inlay. Make two small cones of blue modeling paste for shoes, and mark a heel on each shoe using a sharp knife. On the top of each shoe, make a small indent using the bone tool. Press

the ends of the legs into the indent and affix with a little water. To make buttons, roll some pink modeling paste into three small balls and press onto the body, using the bone tool to indent. Set aside to dry (Figure A).

3. To make the arms, separately roll some yellow and orange modeling paste into two small cones. At the wider end of each cone, press a small indent for the hand. To create the hands, shape two pieces of white modeling paste into small circles and press flat. Cut out a thumb and fingers using a sharp knife. Affix to the wide end of the arms with a little water. Affix the arms to the body using a little water (Figure A).

4. To create the collar, roll out a small piece of blue modeling paste. Cut out a flower shape using the flower cutter. Insert the dry spaghetti into the top of the body, leaving $1/2$ inch protruding from the top. Push the collar onto the protruding piece of

spaghetti and affix to the body using a little water. To make the head, roll some skin color modeling paste into a ball. Push the head onto the spaghetti stick and affix to the collar using a little water. Shape some red modeling paste into a cone-shaped hat. To make the hair, shape two small pieces of yellow modeling paste into semi-circles and press flat. Cut small grooves to create curls and affix to the sides of the head. Roll tiny balls of blue modeling paste into eyes, make a larger ball of red modeling paste into a nose, and add a short sausage of white modeling paste, curled up at the ends, for the mouth.

A

41

Balls

5. To make striped balls, roll some orange modeling paste into a ball. Roll some yellow modeling paste into a thin sausage. Press one end of the sausage onto the top of the ball and wrap it around the ball until you reach the bottom. Gently roll the ball between the palms of your hands to inlay. To make spotted balls, roll some blue modeling paste into a ball. Place tiny balls of yellow modeling paste around the ball and gently roll between the palms of your hands to inlay. Repeat using various color combinations to create a total of 40 balls (Figure B).

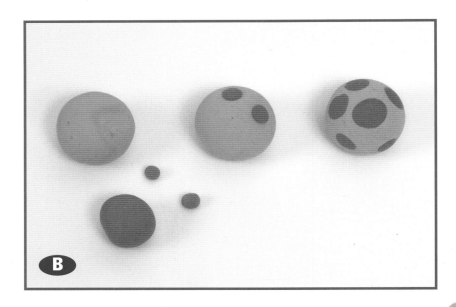

Preparing the cake

6. Level the cake and turn it upside down onto the cake board. Spread buttercream over the top and sides of the cake. Roll out the white rolled fondant and wrap the cake, using the pizza cutter to cut away the excess. Using the open-curve crimper, crimp around the upper edge of the cake (Figure C).

7. Roll the orange modeling paste into a 26 x 2-inch strip. Use the pizza cutter to straighten one length of the strip. Use the frill cutter to create a jagged pattern along the other length. Press the strip around the base of the cake, using a little water to stick.

8. To create the clown's carpet, roll out the green rolled fondant. Place small balls of blue modeling paste on top and gently roll to inlay. Use the crinkled round cutter to cut out the carpet and stick on top of the cake using a little water. Place the clown on the top of the carpet, using a little royal icing to stick (Figure C).

9. Use white royal icing to affix the balls along the top of the cake and around the cake on the cake board (Figure C).

Surf's Up

This cake will draw everyone in from the beach—even when the waves are high. I recommend using a relatively dry recipe for this cake, as this will make it easier to cut the wave shape.

Materials

* **10-inch round cake and 10-inch square cake**
* **3 cups buttercream or smooth cream of your choice**
* **5 pounds rolled fondant, divided and tinted to make:**
  * 3½ pounds sea blue
  * 1½ pounds white
* **13 ounces modeling paste, divided and tinted to make:**
  * 2 ounces yellow
  * 4 ounces orange
  * 2 ounces pink
  * 1 ounce blue
  * 2 ounces green
  * 1 ounce red
  * 1 ounce skin color
* **1 batch of royal icing (page 18), divided into equal parts to make:**
  * white, thick consistency
  * white, thin consistency

Tools

* **Rolling pin**
* **12-inch square cake board**
* **Pizza cutter or sharp knife**
* **Open-curve crimper**
* **Flower cutter**
* **4-inch and 1-inch round cutters**
* **Three 4-inch wooden skewers**
* **3 balls, cut in half or stabilized in cups**
* **Templates (pages 100–103)**
* **Three 1-inch pieces of dry spaghetti**
* **Plastic drinking straw, halved lengthwise**
* **Small paintbrush**
* **Brown gel food color**
* **2 decorating bags and couplers**
* **#2 round decorating tip**
* **#6 star decorating tip**
* **Toothpick**
* **7-inch cardboard round**

One day in advance

Cake board

1. Thinly roll out 12 ounces of sea blue rolled fondant and cover the cake board, trimming the edges with the pizza cutter. Crimp an S-shaped pattern along the edge by alternating the position of the open-curve crimper each time you crimp, and leaving a small space between each pair of crimps. Set aside to dry for at least 12 hours.

Umbrellas

2. To make the umbrellas, roll out 2 ounces of yellow modeling paste. Roll out some orange modeling paste and cut out several flowers using the flower cutter. Place a tiny ball of pink modeling paste in the center of each flower. Place the flowers onto the yellow modeling paste and gently roll to inlay. Cut out a circle using the 4-inch round cutter. Poke a hole in the middle of the circle with a skewer, then mark a vertical line across the middle to divide the surface into halves. Mark again to make four, then eight, equal sections. Using the 1-inch round cutter, cut out a semi-circle from the edge of each section. Gently press the umbrella onto a ball, so that the umbrella takes on a dome shape as it dries (Figure A).

3. Repeat Step 2 using different combinations of the same colors to create three umbrellas. Set aside to dry for 4 hours.

4. After the umbrellas are dry, remove them from the balls and turn upside down. Insert the skewers into the holes, securing with some royal icing. Set aside to dry for 12 hours.

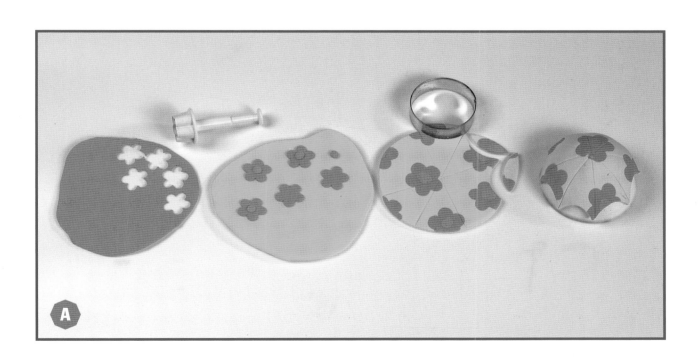

A

Surfer Figure

5. To make the surfer's shirt, roll some red modeling paste into a cone shape. Make two indents near the top of the cone and affix small cones of red modeling paste for sleeves. Insert a piece of raw spaghetti into each sleeve to form a T-shaped support for the arms. Insert a third piece of raw spaghetti that extends upwards from the top of the shirt. This will be used to support the head (Figure B).

6. To make the arms, roll some skin color modeling paste into two thin sausages. Push the arms onto the pieces of spaghetti until they reach the sleeves and affix using a little water. Gently pinch the arms in at the wrists and flatten at the ends. Cut out a thumb using a sharp knife and mark the fingers (Figure B).

7. Make the pants by rolling some orange modeling paste into a long sausage. Fold the sausage in half to make two legs. Fold the legs in half to make knees. Affix the legs to the bottom of the red shirt with some water. Roll some skin color modeling paste

into small oval shapes for the feet and affix to the bottom of the legs (Figure B).

8. Roll some skin color modeling paste into a ball and carefully push onto the piece of spaghetti extending upwards from the shirt. Affix tiny balls of skin color modeling paste for ears and a nose. Use a toothpick to mark the eyes, and make the mouth by indenting the

halved plastic drinking straw. Paint on the hair using the brown gel food color (Figure B).

Surfboard

9. Thinly roll out the green modeling paste. Place a strip of blue modeling paste in the center and gently roll to inlay. Use the template on page 100 to cut out the surfboard and set aside to dry for 5 hours (Figure C).

Beach balls

10. Roll some green modeling paste into a ball. Place tiny balls of blue modeling paste onto the ball and gently roll between the palms of your hands to inlay. Roll some orange modeling paste into a ball. Wrap a thin sausage of yellow modeling paste around the ball and gently roll to inlay. Repeat using different color combinations.

Preparing the cake

Wave

11. Divide the square cake into quarters. You will only need one quarter to make the wave, leaving the other three quarters as spares. Lay one quarter of the cake on a work surface so that the narrow side is facing up. Working with the narrow end at the bottom, use the template on page 101 to cut out a wave shape (Figure D). Cut the cake by gradually shaving away with a sharp, serrated knife (Figure E). When you have finished cutting the cake, place it in an upright position on your work surface.

12. Level the larger cake and turn it upside down onto the cake board. Spread buttercream over the top and sides of the cake. Roll out the remaining sea blue rolled fondant and wrap the cake, using the pizza cutter to cut away the excess. Crimp an S-shaped pattern along the upper edge by alternating the position of the open-curve crimper each time you crimp, and leaving a small space between each pair of crimps.

13. To cover the wave cake, thickly roll out 1 pound of white rolled fondant. Roll the fondant out a little thicker than usual, as this will make it easier to press against the cake's curved surface. Cover the cake with buttercream and wrap with the white rolled fondant, cutting away the excess. Set aside to dry for 1 hour, then carefully place in the center of the larger cake.

14. Roll out the remaining white rolled fondant and, using the templates on pages 102–103, cut out several wave shapes. Affix the waves along the base of the lower cake using a little water.

15. Pipe thick white royal icing around the base of the wave cake using the #6 star decorating tip. Use the #2 round decorating tip to pipe thick royal icing along the top of the waves in the rolled fondant trim. Decorate the S-shaped crimped patterns along the trim of the cake and cake board using thin royal icing, and the #2 round decorating tip. Twist thin sausages of green modeling paste into seaweed and affix around the cake.

16. Carefully place the surfboard onto the wave cake, using royal icing to stick. Using the #6 star decorating tip, pipe thick royal icing around the surfboard. Let dry for a few minutes, then place the surfer figure onto the surfboard, using royal icing to stick.

17. Insert the three umbrellas onto the surface of the larger cake. Place balls on the cake and cake board using royal icing to stick.

Wickedly Wonderful Witch

Materials

* 9-inch round cake
* 2⅔ cups buttercream or smooth cream
* 3 pounds 2 ounces rolled fondant, divided and tinted to make:
  * 14 ounces red
  * 4 ounces yellow
  * 2 pounds light orange
* 2 pounds 3 ounces modeling paste, divided and tinted to make:
  * 3 ounces yellow
  * 4 ounces orange
  * 6 ounces red
  * 2 ounces black
  * 4 ounces light green
  * Tiny amount of white
  * 1 pound dark orange
* 2¼ cups sugar, divided and tinted for sugar molding, to make:
  * ¾ cup red
  * ¾ cup orange
  * ¾ cup yellow
* 1 batch of yellow royal icing (page 18)

Tools

* Rolling pin
* 12-inch square cake board
* Pizza cutter or sharp knife
* Cylinder mold, empty can, or smooth round glass
* Piece of cardboard
* 4-inch and 5-inch crinkled round cutters
* Bone tool
* Small pieces of foam
* 4-inch round cutter
* Templates (pages 104–105)
* Wooden skewer
* 2-inch piece of dry spaghetti
* Decorating bag and coupler
* #2 round decorating tip

One day in advance

Cake board

1. Thinly roll out the red rolled fondant and cover the cake board, trimming the edges with the pizza cutter. Set aside to dry for at least 12 hours.

2. Roll some yellow modeling paste into several small sausage shapes. Inlay strips of orange modeling paste into some of the yellow sausages. Make snake-like coils out of all of the sausages and set aside to dry (Figure A).

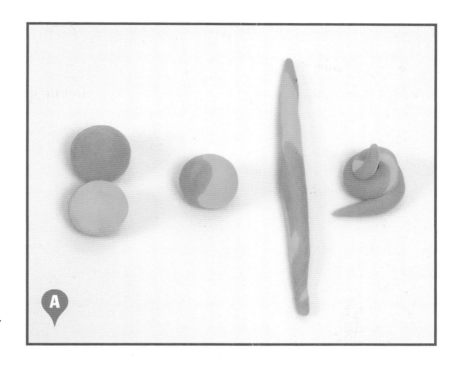

Sugar molding pillar

3. Place the cylinder mold on a clean surface. Pack the red sugar into the mold using a teaspoon. After every two or three spoonfuls, use the back of the spoon to pack the sugar firmly. Continue in this manner until all the red sugar has been packed, then pack the orange and yellow sugar. There is no need for straight lines between the different sugar colors.

4. When the mold is full, run a knife over the surface to level. Place a piece of cardboard over the top and carefully flip over. Gently tap the mold to remove it from the sugar pillar and set aside to set for 12 hours.

5. Thickly roll out 4 ounces of red modeling paste. Cut out a circle using the 4-inch crinkled round cutter and set aside to dry for 12 hours.

Sugar molding pillar

6. To make the body, roll 2 ounces of red modeling paste into a wide-based cone. Roll some orange modeling paste into thin sausages and press horizontally across the front of the body, to form stripes on the shirt. Gently roll to inlay. Using the bone tool, make two indents on the front of the cone for the legs (Figure B).

7. To make the legs, roll some yellow modeling paste into two long sausage shapes, bending them slightly at the knees. Mark the underside of the knees with a sharp knife. Affix the legs to the body using some water to stick. To make the shoes, form two teardrops using black modeling paste. Make a small indent at the wide end of each shoe using the bone tool and affix to the legs with a little water. Place the body on the edge of a surface so that the legs hang off. Place small pieces of foam under the feet to support them while they dry.

8. To make the jacket, roll out the black modeling paste and cut a circle using the 4-inch round cutter. Use the back of a decorating tip to cut out a circle from the center and use the template on page 104 to cut out a triangle from the remaining ring. This is the front of the jacket, were the shirt will show through. Place the jacket on the body and affix using a little water. To make the sleeves, shape two cones out of black modeling paste. Bend at the elbows and mark with a sharp knife.

Indent at the wider ends using the bone tool and affix to the body using a little water. To make the hands, roll some green modeling paste into two balls and flatten slightly. Cut out the thumbs using a sharp knife and mark lines for the fingers. Affix the hands to the ends of the sleeves using a little water (Figure B).

B

9. To make the face, roll 2 ounces of green modeling paste into a ball, pinching in the middle to form a large nose. Use the flat end of the wooden skewer to indent the nostrils and shape the nose around the nostrils. Roll two small pieces of green modeling paste into warts and affix with a little water. Cut the mouth using a sharp knife. To form the eyes, roll small balls of white modeling paste and place smaller balls of black modeling paste on top, for pupils (Figure C).

10. Insert the dry spaghetti into the top of the body, leaving $\frac{1}{2}$ inch protruding from the top. Press the head onto the spaghetti, using a little water to stick. Roll some orange modeling paste into thin strands for hair and place around the top of the head. Shape a brimmed hat used the black modeling paste and stick on top of the head. Set aside to dry (Figure D).

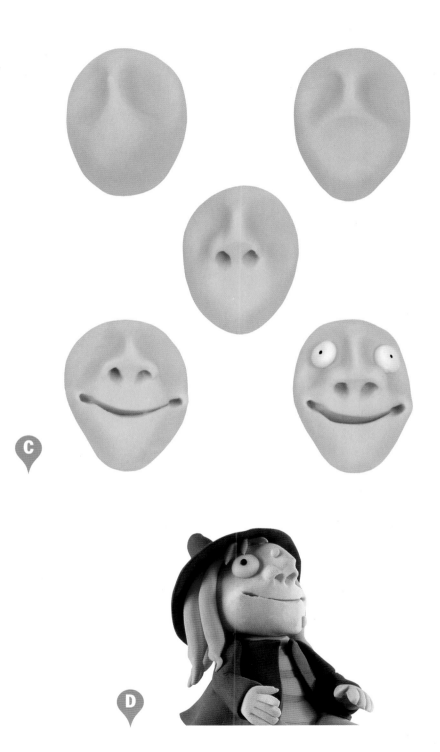

C

D

53

Preparing the cake

11. Level the cake and turn it upside down onto the cake board. Spread buttercream over the top and sides of the cake. Roll out the light orange rolled fondant and wrap the cake, using the pizza cutter to cut away the excess.

12. Roll out the dark orange modeling paste into a 32-inch strip. Straighten one length of the strip using the pizza cutter. Cut a spiked border along the other length using the template on page 105. Affix the straight edge of the strip along the base of the cake, taking care not to stick the spiked edge to the cake. Carefully bend the spikes away from the cake in an uneven manner. Depending on the angle of the spikes, it may be necessary to use small pieces of foam sponge to support the spikes until they dry (Figure E).

13. Roll out the yellow rolled fondant and cut out a circle using the 5-inch crinkled round cutter. Place on the center of the cake and affix

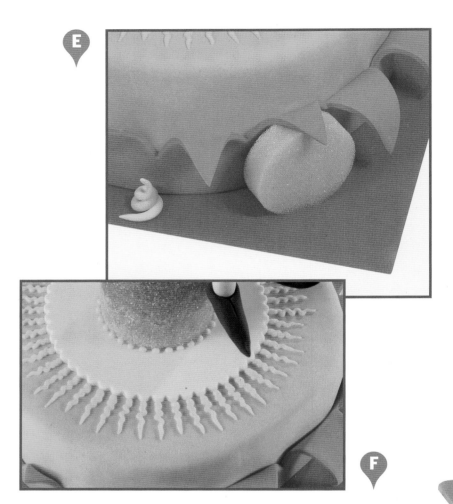

with some water. Use the yellow royal icing to pipe wavy lines extending out of the circle (Figure F).

14. With the yellow end facing down, place the sugar pillar on top of the yellow circle and use some royal icing to stick. Affix the circle of red modeling paste on top of the sugar pillar, using some royal icing to

stick. Place the witch on the red circle, positioning it so that the legs extend off the edge (Figure G).

15. Decorate the base of the pillar with small dots of yellow royal icing. Place the coils of orange and yellow modeling paste on the cake board, using a little royal icing to affix (Figure G).

Happy Birthday to You!

This cake is great for birthdays, or any other occasions when you have something happy to say. Just choose the letters in your message and plan a design that is colorful, creative, and uniquely yours.

Materials

* 9 x 13-inch rectangle cake
* 3 cups buttercream or smooth cream
* 3 pounds 2 ounces rolled fondant, divided and tinted to make:
  * 2½ pounds white
  * 10 ounces red
* 1½ pounds modeling paste, divided and tinted to make:
  * 4 ounces red
  * 4 ounces orange
  * 4 ounces yellow
  * 4 ounces blue
  * 4 ounces green
  * 4 ounces pink
* 2 batches of royal icing (page 18), divided into equal parts and tinted to make:
  * blue
  * red
  * orange
  * yellow
  * green

Tools

* Rolling pin
* Alphabet cutters
* Several 4-inch wooden skewers
* 6 x 28-inch rectangle cake board
* Pizza cutter or sharp knife
* Open-curve crimper
* Bone tool
* Several decorating bags and couplers
* #1.5 round decorating tip

One day in advance

1. Plan your message, and the colors of the letters in your message, on a piece of paper. Be sure to make at least two letters from each color, and take care not to place letters of the same color beside each other. Also, make sure that the cutters you have are small enough so that your message will fit on the cake. For example, if you are writing "Happy Birthday," you will need room for 13 letters on your cake. If the cake is 26 inches long, each letter must be no more than 2 inches wide.

2. Roll out various colors of modeling paste, and cut out the letters in your message using the alphabet cutters. Carefully insert a wooden skewer halfway into each letter, taking care that the skewer does not pierce the front or back of the letter, and leaving 2 inches of the skewer protruding from the bottom. Set aside to dry for 5 hours.

Preparing the cake

3. Level the cake and turn it upside down on a work surface. Cut the cake in half lengthwise so that you have two 4½ x 13-inch strips of cake. Place both halves on the cake board so that the narrow ends of the cakes are side-by-side, forming a 4½ x 26-inch strip of cake.

4. Spread buttercream over the top and sides of the cake. Roll out the white rolled fondant and wrap the cake, using the pizza cutter to cut away the excess.

5. Roll out the red rolled fondant into a 61-inch strip and affix around the base of the cake using some water. You may find it easier to manage several shorter strips, affixing them to each other and to the base of the cake using water. Crimp the fondant using the open-curve crimper.

6. To make the balloons, roll various colors of modeling paste into teardrop shapes. Press the balloons against a work surface to flatten one side and affix a small ball of modeling paste at the narrow part of the balloon. Press the center of the ball using the bone tool. Affix the balloons along the sides of the cake using royal icing. Use blue royal icing to pipe on balloon strings and use various colors to make confetti and streamers (Figures A–B).

7. Gently lay the letters on top of the cake, arranging all of them to make sure they are evenly spaced. When you are satisfied with their layout, carefully insert the wooden skewers into the cake (Figures C–D).

A

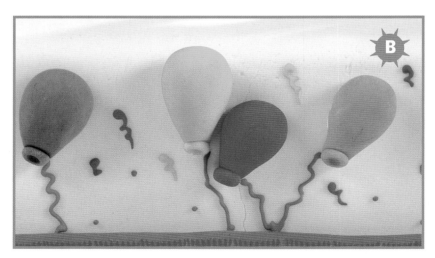

B

58

Spring Is Springing

The snow has melted and the flowers are blooming. Celebrate spring—or any springtime occasion—with this cheerful and colorful cake.

Materials

* **10-inch round cake**
* **1½ cups buttercream or smooth cream**
* **4 pounds 4 ounces rolled fondant, divided and tinted to make:**
  * 1 pound 2 ounces green
  * 2½ pounds white
  * 7 ounces red
  * 1 ounce orange
  * 1 ounce yellow
  * 1 ounce pink
* **10 ounces green modeling paste**
* **2 batches of royal icing (page 18), divided into equal parts and tinted to make:**
  * pink
  * red
  * orange
  * purple
  * yellow

Tools

* **Template (page 106)**
* **Parchment paper**
* **Several decorating bags and couplers**
* **#2 round decorating tip**
* **21 toothpicks, or 4-inch pieces of green floristry wire**
* **Rolling pin**
* **Pizza cutter or sharp knife**
* **12-inch square cake board**
* **Open-curve crimper**
* **6-inch crinkled round cutter**
* **Bone tool**
* **Flower cutter**
* **1 yard purple ribbon**

One day in advance

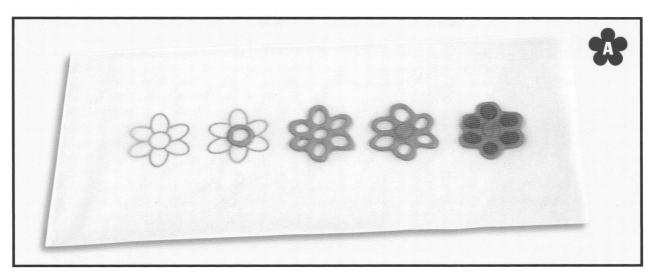

Flowers

1. Trace 21 flowers onto white paper, using the template on page 106. Place the parchment paper over the white paper and re-trace the outline of 7 flowers using the pink royal icing. Repeat using the red and orange royal icing. Wait 10 minutes, then fill in using purple, yellow, and red royal icing. You will need 21 flowers for this cake, but I recommend making a few extra in case any break while you are assembling the cake. Set aside to dry for 12 hours (Figure A).

2. When the flowers are completely dry, remove from the parchment paper and turn over, so that the flat sides are facing up. Using some royal icing, affix a toothpick to each flower, so that a stem of 2½ inches extends from the bottom of each flower. Using different color combinations, pipe royal icing onto the flat sides of the flowers, so that each flower has two fronts. Set aside to dry for 12 hours (Figure B).

Cake board

3. Thinly roll out 12 ounces of green rolled fondant and cover the cake board, trimming the edges with the pizza cutter. Set aside to dry for at least 12 hours.

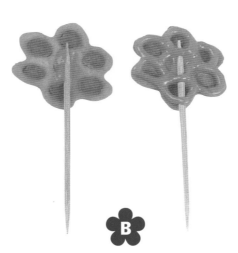

Preparing the cake

4. Level the cake and turn it upside down onto the cake board. Spread buttercream over the top and sides of the cake. Roll out the white rolled fondant and wrap the cake, using the pizza cutter to cut away the excess. Using the open-curve crimper, crimp along the upper edge of the cake.

5. Roll out 6 ounces of green rolled fondant and cut out a circle with the crinkled round cutter. Affix on top of the cake using a little water and indent each crinkle using the bone tool (Figure C).

6. To make the leaves, roll the remaining green modeling paste into 21 sausage shapes. Gently pinch both ends of each sausage so that it tapers to a point, then fold in the middle to form a pair of leaves. Bend the end of each leaf outwards. Place the leaves onto the green circle using a little water. In the center of each pair of leaves, insert the stem of a prepared flower (Figure D).

7. Roll the red rolled fondant into a 32-inch sausage and wrap around the base of the cake, using water to stick. Crimp the fondant using the open-curve crimper (Figure D).

8. Thinly roll out the orange, yellow, and pink rolled fondant. Cut out 7 flowers from each color using the flower cutter. Stick the flowers onto the cake board using a little water. Place a dot in the center of each flower using a contrasting color of royal icing (Figure D).

9. Pipe small hearts at regular intervals around the top of the cake with yellow royal icing. Decorate the crimped rim of the cake using orange royal icing. Also use the orange royal icing to pipe small dots along the crimped border at the base of the cake (Figure D).

10. Affix the ribbon around the center of the cake using royal icing (Figure D).

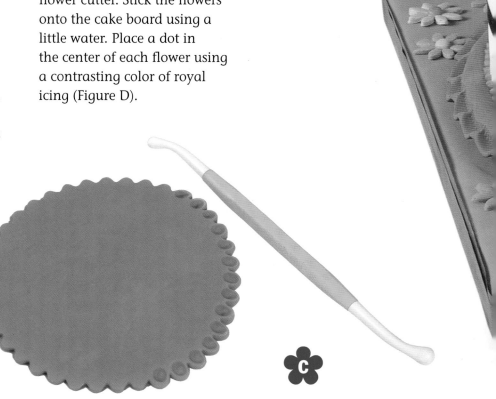

Sally Says "Surprise!"

This is an unforgettable way of saying "Surprise!" "Congratulations!" or "Best Wishes!" It includes templates for boy and girl figures.

Materials

* 10 x 3-inch round cake and 6 x 2-inch round cake
* 3 cups buttercream
* 5 pounds 10 ounces rolled fondant, divided and tinted to make:
  * 3½ pounds white
  * 14 ounces light blue
  * 6 ounces purple
  * 8 ounces red
  * 6 ounces orange
* 1 pound 5 ounces modeling paste, divided and tinted to make:
  * 3 ounces green
  * 3 ounces purple
  * 3 ounces red
  * 3 ounces orange
  * 3 ounces yellow
  * 3 ounces pink
  * 3 ounces blue
* 2 batches of royal icing (page 18), divided into equal parts and tinted to make:
  * white
  * skin color
  * orange
  * red
  * pink
  * blue
  * green

Tools

* Templates (pages 107–108)
* Parchment paper
* Several decorating bags and couplers
* #2 and #4 round decorating tips
* 2 wooden skewers
* Star cutter
* Heart cutter
* Thirty 8-inch pieces green floristry wire
* Rolling pin
* Pizza cutter or sharp knife
* 12-inch square cake board
* Open-curve crimper
* 9-inch plate
* 7-inch crinkled round cutter
* 6-inch cardboard round

Three days in advance

Boy or girl figure

1. Trace a boy or girl figure onto white paper, using the templates on pages 107–108. I recommend making two identical figures, so that you have a spare in case one breaks when you assemble the cake. Place the parchment paper over the white paper and re-trace the figure using white royal icing. Wait a few minutes, then fill in with various colors of royal icing, according to the photograph or your own design. First fill in background colors for the banner, face, and clothes. Set aside for 1 hour, then pipe in the message on the banner, details on the face, and patterns on the clothes. Set aside for 24 hours to dry (Figures A–B).

Two days in advance

Boy or girl figure

2. When the figures are completely dry, carefully remove them from the parchment paper and turn over, so that the flat sides are facing up. Starting from the neck and extending 2 inches below the feet, affix a wooden skewer to each figure with some royal icing. Trace the outlines of the figures onto the back using white royal icing. Wait a few minutes, then fill in background colors so that both sides of the figures are identical. Wait 1 hour, then pipe in details. Set aside to dry for 24 hours (Figure C).

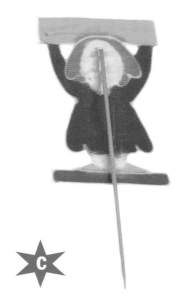

Stars and hearts

3. Make various patterns of hearts and stars by following these general guidelines: For the spotted green heart, thickly roll out some green modeling paste. The modeling paste should be thick enough so that you can insert floristry wire into the modeling paste without damaging its surface. Place tiny balls of purple modeling paste onto the green and gently roll to inlay. Cut out a heart using the heart cutter. Carefully insert a piece of floristry wire partway up the heart. Repeat using various color combinations to create 15 stars and 15 hearts, of various sizes and patterns. Set aside to dry (Figure D).

Preparing the cake

4. Level the larger cake and turn it upside down onto the cake board. Spread buttercream over the top and sides of the cake. Roll out 2½ pounds of white rolled fondant and wrap the cake, covering the top and sides and cutting away the excess with the pizza cutter. Using the open-curve crimper, crimp along the upper edge of the cake.

5. Roll out 7 ounces of light blue rolled fondant and place the plate on top. Cut out a large circle by running a sharp knife along the edge of the plate. Place the circle on top of the cake, using a little water to affix.

6. Level the smaller cake and turn it upside down onto the cardboard round. Cover with buttercream and wrap with the remaining white rolled fondant, cutting away the excess.

7. Place the smaller cake on top of the larger cake, leaving the cardboard round between the two cakes.

8. Roll out the purple rolled fondant and cut out a circle using the crinkled round cutter. Place on top of the smaller cake, taking care so that the edge of the circle hangs evenly around the cake. Affix with some water and set aside to dry for 1 hour.

9. Roll the remaining light blue rolled fondant into a 19-inch sausage and wrap around the base of the upper cake, using water to stick.

10. Decorate the crimped edge of the lower cake with green royal icing and use red royal icing to pipe small hearts, at regular intervals, around the lower cake.

11. Carefully insert the figure into the center of the upper cake, pushing it in until the skewers cannot be seen (Figure E).

12. Make coiled stems on 7 hearts and 7 stars by tightly wrapping the stems around a pencil. Remove the wire from the pencil by slipping it over the top, so that the wire retains the coiled shape. Insert the shapes along the top of the lower cake, alternating between coiled and straight stems (Figure E).

13. Roll the red rolled fondant into a thick, 33-inch sausage and wrap around the base of the lower cake, using water to stick. Roll the orange rolled fondant into a thinner 32-inch sausage and wrap it around the base of the lower cake, placing it along the upper edge of the red sausage. Use a little water to stick (Figure F).

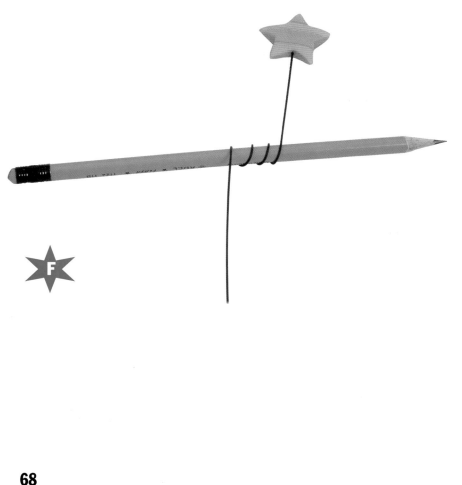

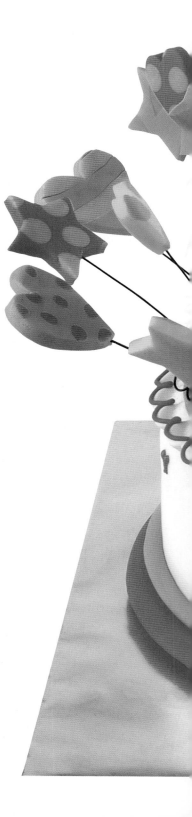

Paradise of Purses

Perfect for the person who loves to shop 'til they drop, this cake is sure to revive anyone who has spent a busy day at the mall.

Materials

* 8-inch round cake
* 1½ cups buttercream or smooth cream
* 1½ pounds white rolled fondant
* 1 pound 10 ounces modeling paste, divided and tinted to make:
  * 2 ounces red
  * 2 ounces yellow
  * 1 ounce pink
  * 11 ounces purple
  * 6 ounces green
  * 2 ounces orange
  * 2 ounces blue
* 1 batch of royal icing (page 18), divided into equal parts and tinted to make:
  * orange
  * yellow

Tools

* Design wheeler
* Toothpick
* 2 decorating bags and couplers
* #1 and #2 round decorating tip
* Sharp knife
* Rolling pin
* Small flower cutter
* 10-inch round cake board
* Pizza cutter or sharp knife
* Open-curve crimper
* Lined rolling pin
* Small heart cutter
* 6-inch crinkled round cutter
* 26-inch red ribbon

Red purse

1. Roll some red modeling paste into a ball and flatten on one side. Use the design wheeler to mark a seam along the edge of the purse. Form a button with yellow modeling paste and mark around the edges using a toothpick. Make a handle from pink modeling paste. Use orange royal icing to pipe small spikes on the purse (Figures A–B).

Purple purse

2. Shape some purple modeling paste into a rectangle that is slightly rounded at one end. Lay a thin strip of red modeling paste over the top of the rounded end. Using the #2 decorating tip, pipe a small button of orange royal icing on each side of the strip. Using the #1 decorating tip, decorate with tiny dots of yellow royal icing. Use orange modeling paste to make the handle (Figure B).

Yellow and blue purse

3. Shape some yellow modeling paste into a small cube. Mark along the middle using a sharp knife. Cut two small rectangles of blue modeling paste and stick on one side of the purse. Use purple modeling paste to form four small buttons and a handle (Figure B).

Yellow and pink purse

4. Roll some yellow modeling paste into a ball and flatten on one side. Use the design wheeler to mark a seam along the edge of the purse. Add a small rectangle of pink modeling paste over the top, and mark a seam using the design wheeler. Using the #2 tip, pipe four small buttons

with orange royal icing, and add a tiny piece of purple modeling paste for the handle (Figure B).

Blue purse

5. Shape some blue modeling paste into a rectangle that is slightly narrower at one end. Mark a seam around the edge using the design wheeler. Roll out some green modeling paste and cut out two flowers using the flower cutter. Place a flower on either side of the purse, using a little water to stick. Add a dot of yellow royal icing in the center of each flower. Shape two thin handles

using green modeling paste and affix on the top of the purse. Use a toothpick to mark buttons (Figure B).

Pink wallet

6. Shape some pink modeling paste into a small rectangle. Roll out some orange modeling paste and cut a small piece to form a flap. Roll out some purple modeling paste and cut out a flower using the flower cutter. Place the flower on the wallet, and add a dot of yellow royal icing in the center (Figure B).

Set aside all of the purses to dry for 1 hour.

71

Preparing the cake

7. Level the cake and turn it upside down onto the cake board. Spread buttercream over the top and sides of the cake. Roll out the white rolled fondant and wrap the cake, using the pizza cutter to cut away the excess. Using the open-curve crimper, crimp along the upper edge of the cake.

8. Roll the purple modeling paste into a 26 x 1½-inch strip. Re-roll once using the lined rolling pin and straighten the edges using the pizza cutter. Affix around the base of the cake using a little water. Add dots of orange royal icing along the top of the strip at regular intervals.

9. Roll out the remaining orange modeling paste. Re-roll once using the lined rolling pin (Figure C), then cut out hearts using the heart cutter.

10. Roll out the green modeling paste and cut out a circle with the crinkled round cutter. Affix on the top of the cake using a little water. Indent each crinkle using the bone tool and place a dot of yellow royal icing in each indent (Figure D).

11. Affix the ribbon around the bottom of the cake using a few drops of royal icing. Place the purses on top of the cake using a little royal icing to stick.

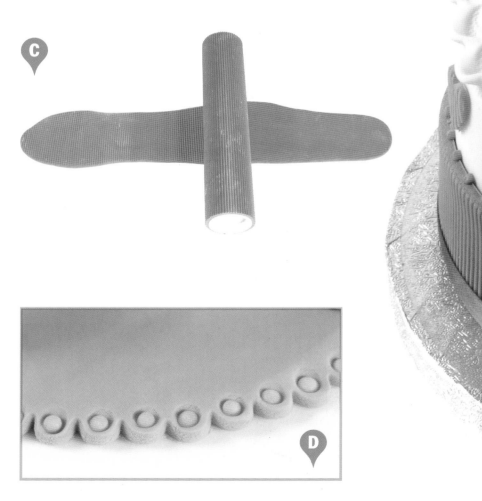

C

D

Heart-to-Heart-to-Heart

There are many ways to say "I love you"—this cake is one of them. Unique and eye-catching, it leaves no doubt where your heart is.

Materials

* 10 x 3-inch round cake and 6 x 2-inch round cake
* 3 cups buttercream
* 5 pounds 2 ounces rolled fondant, divided and tinted to make:
  * 3½ pounds white
  * 7 ounces yellow
  * 6 ounces orange
  * 5 ounces red
  * 1 ounce purple
  * 7 ounces pink
* 14 ounces modeling paste, divided and tinted to make:
  * 2 ounces orange
  * 2 ounces red
  * 2 ounces yellow
  * 2 ounces pink
  * 2 ounces blue
  * 2 ounces green
  * 2 ounces purple

Tools

* Rolling pin
* Heart cutters, various sizes
* Several long wooden skewers
* 12-inch round cake board
* Open-curve crimper
* 9-inch plate
* Sharp knife
* 6-inch cardboard round, with a 2-inch circle cut out of the center
* 5-inch round cutter

One day in advance

Heart beads

1. Thickly roll out 1 ounce of orange modeling paste. The modeling paste should be thick enough so that you can insert a wooden skewer through the modeling paste without damaging its surface. Place a few balls of red modeling paste onto the orange and gently roll to inlay (Figure A).

2. Cut out a heart using a heart cutter. Insert a wooden skewer into the base of the heart, twisting it gently as you push it through the heart, so that the skewer comes out cleanly at the top of the heart (Figure B).

3. Leave the skewer inside the heart as it dries, twisting the skewer every hour so that the modeling paste doesn't stick. Let dry for at least 4 hours.

4. Repeat Steps 1 to 3 using various color combinations to create smaller and larger hearts. Set aside to dry for 4 hours.

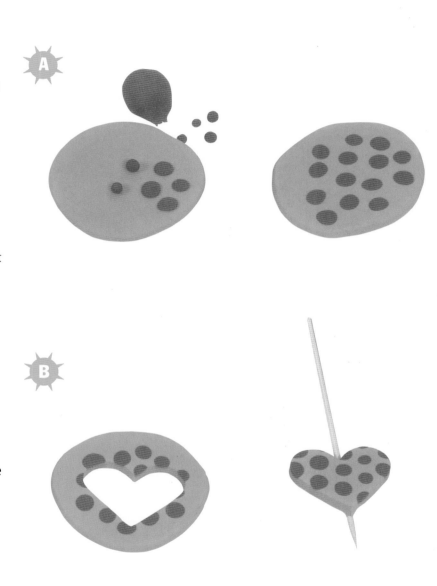

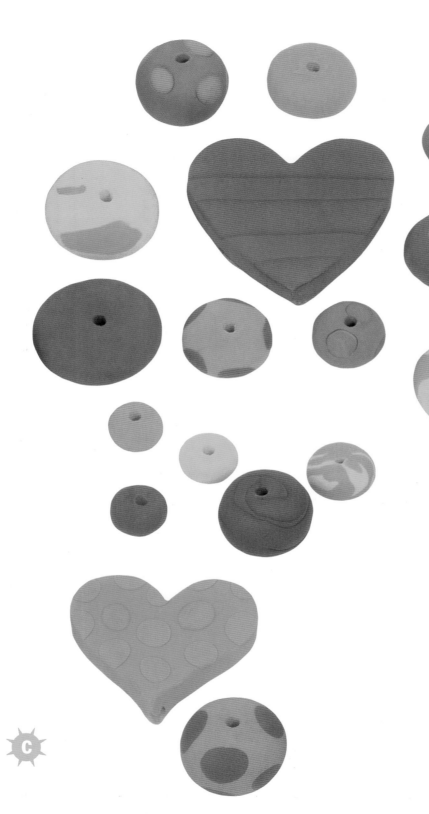

5. Make spotted and striped beads by following these general guidelines: To create a spotted bead, roll some blue modeling paste into a ball. Roll several tiny balls of pink modeling paste and press them onto the blue ball. Roll the ball gently between the palms of your hands to inlay. Insert a wooden skewer into the center of the ball, twisting it gently as you push it through so that the paste doesn't stick to the skewer. To create a

striped bead, wrap a thin sausage of yellow modeling paste around a ball of red modeling paste and gently roll to inlay. Insert a wooden skewer into the center of the ball, twisting it gently as you push it through so that the paste doesn't stick to the skewer. To create oval beads, simply press the spotted or striped bead between your fingers before inserting the skewer. Set aside to dry for 4 hours.

6. Create a variety of striped and spotted beads (Figure C). The amount of beads you need to fill your skewer will depend upon the length of your skewer and the size of the beads. The longer the skewer, the more dramatic the effect, so try to use the longest skewer available.

Put extra beads in a small glass bowl beside your cake and invite guests to create their own designs on the skewer.

Preparing the cake

7. Level the larger cake and turn it upside down onto the cake board. Spread buttercream over the top and sides of the cake. Roll out 2½ pounds of white rolled fondant and wrap the cake, covering the top and sides and cutting away the excess. Using the open-curve crimper, crimp around the upper edge of the cake.

8. Roll out the yellow rolled fondant. Place several small balls of orange rolled fondant onto the yellow and gently roll to inlay. Place the plate on top of the rolled surface and cut out a large circle by running a sharp knife along the edge of the

plate. Place the circle on top of the cake, using a little water to stick.

9. Level the smaller cake and turn it upside down onto the cardboard round. Ensure that the cardboard round is centered, because the skewer must go through the hole in the cardboard, and penetrate the lower cake, in order to support the tower of beads. Cover with buttercream and wrap with the remaining white rolled fondant. Place the smaller cake on top of the larger cake, leaving the cardboard round between the two cakes. Set aside to dry for 1 hour (Figure D).

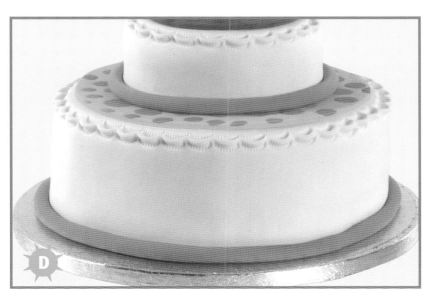

10. Roll out the red rolled fondant. Place several small balls of purple rolled fondant onto the red and gently roll to inlay. Cut out a circle using the round cutter. Place on top of the upper cake and affix with a little water (Figure E).

11. Roll the pink modeling paste into a 32-inch sausage and place around the base of the lower cake, using a little water to stick. Roll the orange rolled fondant into a 19-inch sausage and place around the base of the upper cake, using a little water to stick (Figure E).

12. Gently push the wooden skewer into the center of the top cake until it reaches the cake board. If using a foam cake board, try to pierce the cake board with the skewer, as this will provide extra support. Place the beads and hearts onto the skewer according to your own design (Figure E).

Happily Ever After

The happiest day of a person's life certainly deserves the happiest cake ever. This design will bring a smile to the face of every bride and groom—and each one of their guests.

Materials

* 10-inch round cake and 8-inch round cake
* 3 cups buttercream or smooth cream
* 6 pounds rolled fondant, divided and tinted to make:
  * 5 pounds 12 ounces white
  * 4 ounces red
* 2 pounds 4 ounces modeling paste, divided and tinted to make:
  * 5 ounces grey
  * 2 ounces skin color
  * 9 ounces white
  * 3 ounces black
  * 1 ounce brown
  * Tiny amount of blue (optional)
  * 6 ounces orange
  * 5 ounces yellow
  * 5 ounces red
* 2 batches of royal icing (page 18), divided into equal parts and tinted to make:
  * white
  * red
  * pink
  * purple
  * orange
  * yellow

Tools

* Rolling pin
* 12-inch square cake board
* Wooden skewer
* Templates (pages 109–110)
* Plastic drinking straw, halved lengthwise
* 2-inch piece of dry spaghetti
* Miniature flower plunger cutter
* Several decorating bags and couplers
* #2 round decorating tip
* 8-inch cardboard round
* 5-inch crinkled round cutter

One day in advance

Cake board

1. Thinly roll out 14 ounces of white rolled fondant. Cover the cake board with the rolled fondant, trimming the edges with the pizza cutter. Set aside to dry for at least 12 hours.

Groom figure

2. To make the body, roll the grey modeling paste into a 6-inch cylinder shape. Put aside a pinch of grey modeling paste for the bowtie. Flatten the cylinder slightly and mark a line in the center, from the middle to the bottom, for the legs. Push a wooden skewer through the cylinder so that it protrudes 3 inches below and $1/2$ inch above. To make the neck, roll a small cylinder of skin color modeling paste and stick onto the skewer, ensuring that some of the skewer still protrudes to support the head (Figure A).

3. To make the shirt, shape some white modeling paste into a thin triangle and press onto the top of the body. Mark a line down the middle of the shirt with a knife and shape two tiny triangles for the collar. Form the bowtie by making a tiny sausage of grey modeling paste, flattening it slightly, and twisting it in the middle (Figure A).

4. To make the suit, thinly roll out the black modeling paste and cut according to the templates on page 109. Affix the pieces onto the body using some water. To make the sleeves, roll two pieces of black modeling paste into sausage shapes that taper out slightly at one end. Indent the wider ends using the bone tool. Bend the sleeves slightly and use a sharp knife to mark elbows. Affix the narrower ends of the sleeves to the suit (Figure A).

5. To make the hands, shape some skin color modeling paste into teardrops and flatten. Cut the thumbs using a sharp knife and mark the fingers. Stick the hands onto the ends of the sleeves using a little water (Figure A).

6. Roll some black modeling paste into two oval shapes for the shoes, marking the center of each shoe with a toothpick (Figure A).

7. Roll some skin color modeling paste into an oval to form the head. Carefully press the head onto the skewer and affix using a little water. Use tiny amounts of skin color modeling paste to form the nose and ears, and tiny balls of blue modeling paste to form the eyes. If you don't have blue modeling paste for the eyes, brown or black is fine, too. Mark the smile by indenting the halved plastic drinking straw. Roll some sausages of brown modeling paste to form the hair and stick on top of the head (Figure A).

Bride figure

8. To make the body, roll 6 ounces of white modeling paste into a wide-based cone. Gently form a waist about $^4/_5$ of the way up from the bottom of the cone, and mold a bust and neckline. This technique requires a very gentle touch and may take some practice. To form the skirt, thinly roll out 3 ounces of white modeling paste and cut according to the template on page 110. Affix the skirt around the bride's hips using some water and decorate with dots of white royal icing (Figure B).

9. Insert the piece of dry spaghetti into the top of the body, leaving $^1/_2$ inch protruding. Roll a ball of skin color modeling paste and push onto the piece of spaghetti to form the neck and collar area. Gently press the modeling paste down so that it meets the neckline of the dress, using a little water to stick. Pipe small dots of white royal icing along the edge of the dress (Figure B).

10. To make arms, shape two thin sausages of skin color modeling paste. Indent each sausage gently near one end to form the wrist, and flatten the end slightly to form the hand. Cut out a thumb using a sharp knife and mark the fingers. Gently bend near the middle to form elbows and affix to the sides of the body (Figure B).

11. To make the head, shape an oval with some skin color modeling paste. Carefully press the head onto the skewer and affix using a little water. Form the nose using a tiny ball of skin color modeling paste, and make eyes using tiny balls of blue modeling paste. Mark the smile by indenting the halved plastic drinking straw. Roll some orange modeling paste into sausages to form the hair and stick on top of the head. Using the flower plunger cutter, cut out four flowers from the white modeling paste and place in a band over the hair (Figure B).

Love cards

12. Thinly roll out 5 ounces each of orange, yellow, and red modeling paste. Cut out 11 rectangles measuring 1½ x 2½ inches from each color. Using the photo as a guide, decorate the cards with royal icing, using various combinations of colors and designs. The designs do not need to be identical, but there should be an equal number of heart and flower designs (Figure C).

Preparing the cake

13. Level the larger cake and turn it upside down onto the cake board. Spread buttercream over the top and sides of the cake. Roll out 2½ pounds white rolled fondant and wrap the cake, using the pizza cutter to cut away the excess.

14. Level the smaller cake and turn it upside down onto the cardboard round. Cover with buttercream and wrap with white rolled fondant, cutting away the excess. Roll out the red rolled fondant and cut a circle using the crinkled round cutter. Place on top of the smaller cake, using a little water to stick.

15. Place the smaller cake on top of the larger cake, leaving the cardboard round between the two cakes. Set aside for 1 hour to dry.

16. Roll a thick 26-inch sausage from the white rolled fondant and affix around the base of the upper cake using a little water. Roll a

thick 32-inch sausage from the remaining white rolled fondant and affix around the base of the lower cake.

17. Place the love cards around the base of each cake, alternating between heart and flower cards, and using a little royal icing at the top and bottom of each

card to stick. Pipe hearts in the corners of the cake board using orange and yellow royal icing.

18. Place the bride and groom side-by-side on the center of the upper cake and make sure to completely insert the skewer supporting the groom (Figure D).

Smiling Boy

The following two designs can be created on their own, or as a set. They are perfect for twins' birthdays, anniversaries, or any other occasion in which two people are celebrating a special day together.

Materials

* 9-inch round cake
* 2⅔ cups buttercream or smooth cream of your choice
* 3 pounds 7 ounces rolled fondant, divided and tinted to make:
  * 2 pounds white
  * 1 pound skin color
  * 7 ounces blue
* 11 ounces modeling paste, divided and tinted to make:
  * 1 ounce red
  * 7 ounces yellow
  * 3 ounces light green

Tools

* 12-inch round cake board
* Rolling pin
* Pizza cutter or sharp knife
* Template (page 111)
* Bone tool
* Sharp knife

Preparing the cake

1. Level the cake and turn it upside down onto the cake board. Spread buttercream over the top and sides of the cake. Roll out the white rolled fondant and wrap the cake, using the pizza cutter to cut away the excess.

2. Using white rolled fondant, form two small balls and a small sausage. These pieces will form the cheeks and nose that protrude from the face. Gently place the pieces onto the surface of the cake. You will probably need to adjust the location of these pieces several times, so make sure they don't stick onto the cake (Figure A).

3. Thinly roll out the skin color rolled fondant and cut out a face shape, using the template on page 111. Gently place the face onto the cake, laying it over the cheeks and nose. Adjust the underlying pieces so that the cheeks and nose protrude in the right places (Figure B). Make sure you have enough space below the chin to place the bowtie.

4. Once the pieces are in the right place, use the bone tool to poke nostrils and gently shape the nose. Use the bone tool to smooth around the nose and cheeks to bring them out. Cut the mouth using the sharp knife, and gently open to form a smile (Figure C). Place a small strip of thinly rolled red modeling paste inside the mouth.

5. When you are satisfied with the location and form of all the features, apply a little water to the underside of the face, lifting one section at a time.

A

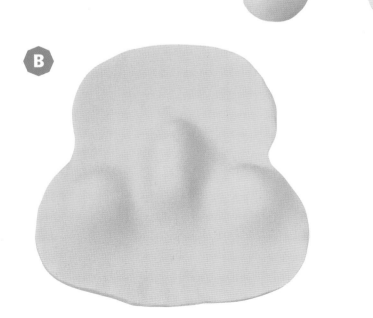

B

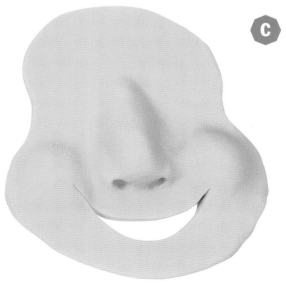

C

6. Roll the yellow modeling paste into sausage shapes of varying lengths to form the hair. Arrange around the top of the face, allowing some pieces to extend beyond the edge of the cake, and using a little water to stick (Figure D).

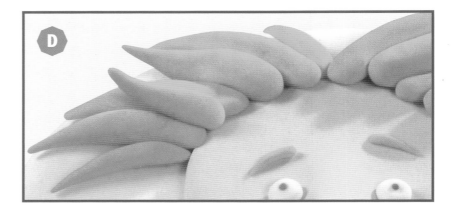

7. To make the bowtie, roll out the light green modeling paste. Place thin sausages of blue rolled fondant on top and gently roll to inlay. Cut a 2 x 5-inch rectangle and pinch in the middle. Place a strip of blue rolled fondant over the middle, using a little water to stick (Figure E). Place the bowtie onto the top of the cake, using a little water to stick.

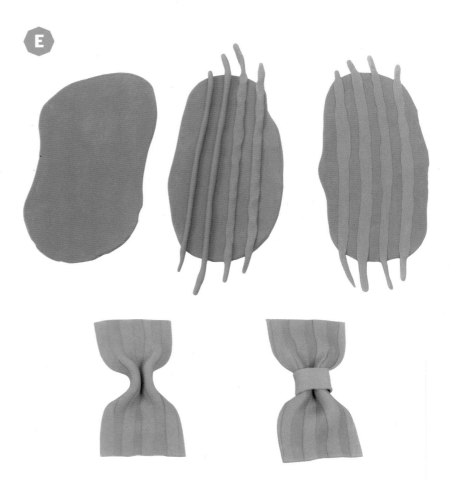

8. Use some yellow modeling paste to form eyebrows, and some skin color rolled fondant to form ears. Roll two small balls of white rolled fondant into eyes and roll two tiny balls of blue rolled fondant into pupils.

9. Roll the remaining blue rolled fondant into a 29-inch sausage and wrap around the base of the cake, using water to stick.

Smiling Girl

Materials

* 9-inch round cake
* 2⅔ cups buttercream or smooth cream of your choice
* 3 pounds 5 ounces rolled fondant, divided and tinted to make:
  * 2 pounds white
  * 1 pound skin color
  * 5 ounces purple
* 1 pound 1 ounce modeling paste, divided and tinted to make:
  * 1 ounce red
  * 12 ounces orange
  * 1 ounce purple
  * 2 ounces yellow
  * 1 ounce pink
  * Tiny amount of blue

Tools

* Rolling pin
* Pizza cutter or sharp knife
* 12-inch round cake board
* Template (page 111)
* Bone tool

Preparing the cake

1. Level the cake and turn it upside down onto the cake board. Spread buttercream over the top and sides of the cake. Roll out the white rolled fondant and wrap the cake, using the pizza cutter to cut away the excess.

2. Using white rolled fondant, form two small balls and a small sausage. These pieces will form the cheeks and nose that protrude from the face. Gently place the pieces onto the surface of the cake. You will probably need to adjust the location of these pieces several times, so make sure they don't stick onto the cake (Figure A).

3. Thinly roll out the skin color rolled fondant and cut out a face shape using the template on page 111. Gently place the face onto the cake, laying it over the cheeks and nose. Adjust the underlying pieces so that the cheeks and nose protrude in the right places (Figure B). Make sure you have enough space below the chin to place the collar.

4. Once the pieces are in the right place, use the bone tool to poke nostrils and gently shape the nose. Use the bone tool to smooth around the nose and cheeks to bring them out. Cut the mouth using the sharp knife, and open to form a smile (Figure C). Roll out some white rolled fondant into a strip that will fit inside the mouth. Mark teeth onto the strip using a knife and insert into the open mouth.

5. When you are satisfied with the location and form of all the features, apply a little water to the underside of the face, lifting one section at a time.

A

B

C
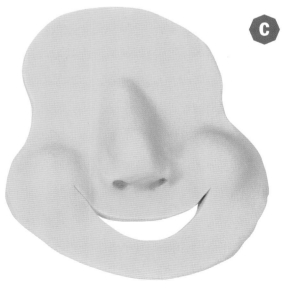

6. Roll a thin sausage of red modeling paste that tapers at the ends for the bottom lip and roll two thin teardrop shapes for the top lip. Stick the lips onto the face using a little water (Figure D).

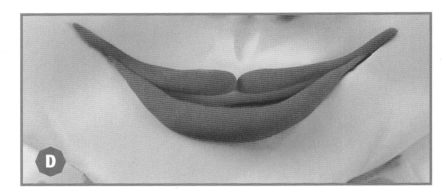

7. To make the hair, roll the orange modeling paste into several long sausage shapes. Arrange the hair into two pigtails, allowing some pieces of hair to extend beyond the edge of the cake. Use a little water to stick. Make ribbons using the purple modeling paste and place on the pigtails (Figure E).

8. To make the collar, roll out the yellow modeling paste. Place small balls of pink modeling paste on top and gently roll to inlay. Cut out the collar and stick onto the cake, just below the chin.

9. Use some orange modeling paste to form eyebrows. Roll two small balls of white rolled fondant into eyes and roll two tiny balls of blue modeling paste into pupils.

10. Roll the purple rolled fondant into a 29-inch sausage and wrap around the base of the cake, using water to stick.

Templates

Cheerful Chicks

Chick

Beautiful Baby Birthday

Heart

Colorful and Crazy

Heart

Several sizes of stars

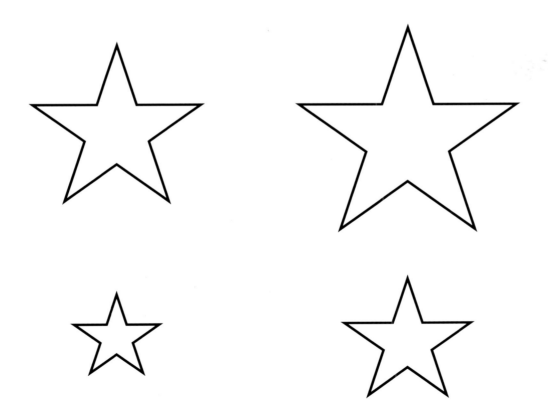

Surf's Up

Surfboard

Surf's Up (continued)

Wave cake

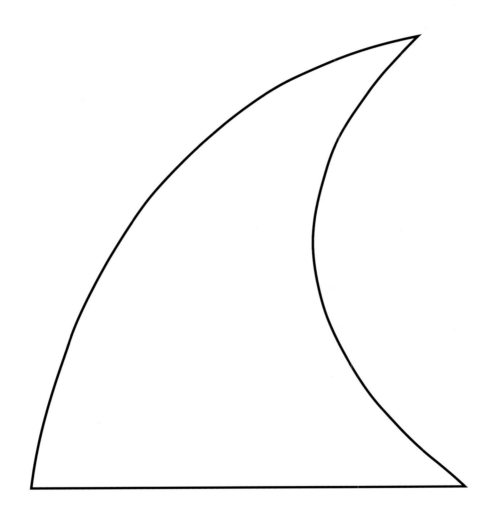

Surf's Up (continued)

Wave cake

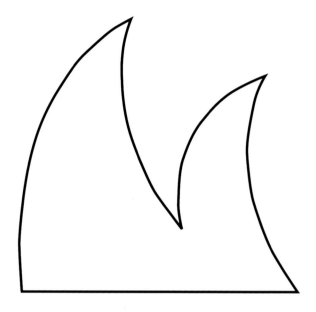

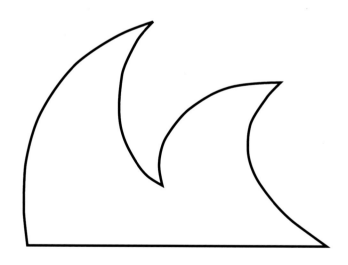

Surf's Up (continued)

Waves of rolled fondant

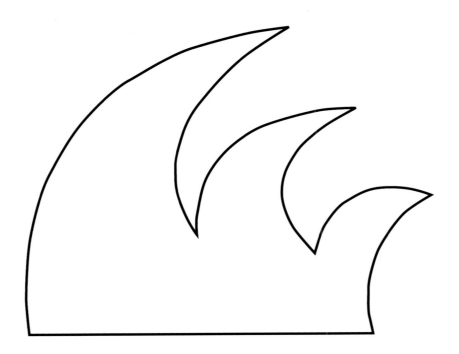

Wickedly Wonderful Witch

Witch's jacket

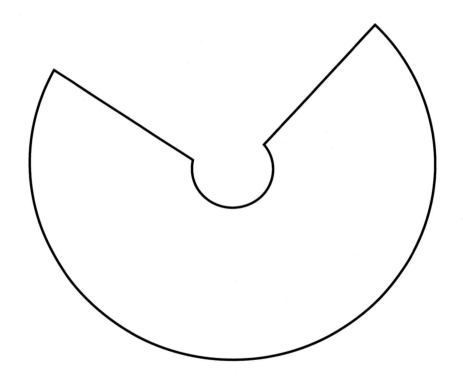

Wickedly Wonderful Witch (continued)

Spiked border along the bottom of the cake

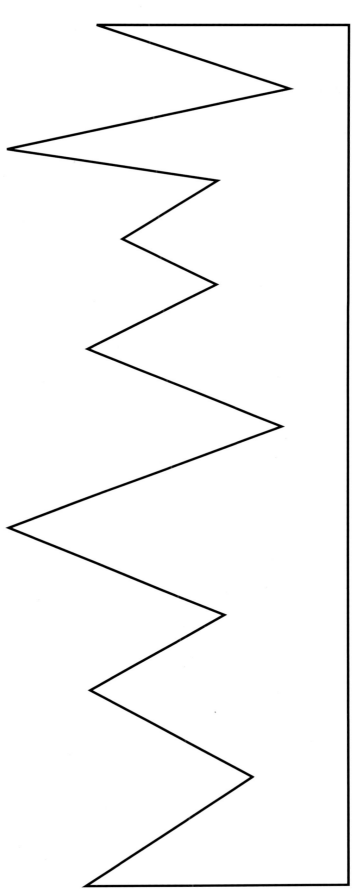

Spring Is Springing

Flower

Sally Says "Surprise!"

Boy figure

Sally Says "Surprise!" (continued)

Girl figure

Happily Ever After

Pieces of groom's suit

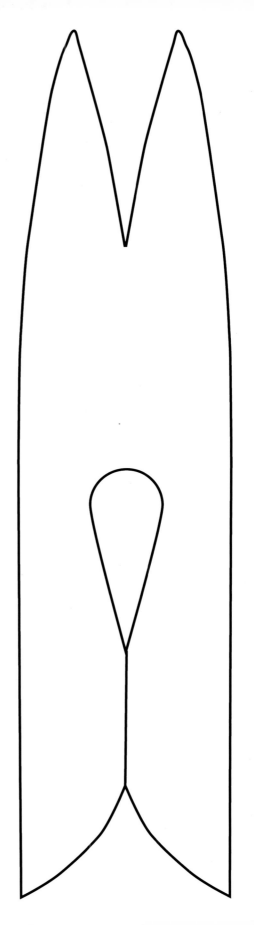

109

Happily Ever After
(continued)

Bride's skirt

Smiling Boy and Smiling Girl

Face shape

Index